YOU ARE ENOUGH

YOU ARE ENOUGH

Always have been . . . Always will be

DAVID J. WALKER

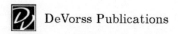 DeVorss Publications

FIRST EDITION, 2007

DeVorss & Company, Publisher
P.O. Box 1389
Camarillo CA 93011-1389
www.devorss.com

Printed in the United States of America

Library of Congress Cataloging-in-Publication Data

Walker, David J., 1940-
  You are enough : always have been, always will be / David J. Walker.
-- 1st DeVorss ed.
    p. cm.
  ISBN 978-0-87516-826-5
1. Self-perception. 2. Self-talk. 3. Affirmations. I. Title.

BF697.5.S43W35 2007
299'.93--dc22

                                                2007008266

This book is dedicated to

Ernest Holmes

Robert Bitzer

and

Cooper Neal

... with added thanks to Gary Peattie
for having faith in *You Are Enough*.

Before You Begin:

Everyone knows how important self-talk is. Self-talk is the means we have of talking ourselves into or out of something. I have included some very simple self-talk exercises at the end of most of the chapters in this book. I invite you to use them to talk yourself into a better life.

Just remember, you are not talking to someone else. You are talking to yourself.

CONTENTS

YOU ARE ENOUGH

Always have been ... Always will be

"Life is bigger than the philosophy,
teaching, or religion that attempts
to explain it. You are life."

– DAVID J. WALKER

FIRST WORDS

WHEN HE WENT INTO MILITARY SERVICE, he went in as an enlisted man. For the first time in his life, he was thrown in with many kinds of people, many of whom he did not respect, let alone admire.

If someone asked him what his life was like before the military, most often he found it necessary to use the power of embellishment, so he could paint a picture that was much better that it actually was. He came very close to describing his parents as the King and Queen of England, and his home as a castle.

He gave the impression (he hoped) of a young man who was far too intelligent and sophisticated to be an enlisted man. It's interesting that this man cared so much about what people thought of him, even people he did not admire or respect.

This young man thought that when you added up everything from his past, it didn't amount to much, which meant that he didn't amount to much, so he proceeded to create a fictional past in hopes that it would command respect, maybe even his own.

I know how this man felt, because this young man was me. I was the one who needed to feel that I amounted to something and I still do. I still need to know that I amount to something. What's different is the way I fulfill this need.

At one time I thought that to feel I amounted to something, I had to be able to remember a wonderful past or at least something great about the present, I have since learned that I only need to remember who *I* am.

Sunday's child, that's me. I was born on March 3, 1940 in Flower Hospital, Toledo, Ohio. My parents were Polish and only Polish on both sides. My first few years were spent growing up in a Polish neighborhood, going to a Polish parochial school. Neither of my grandparents spoke English, and since I didn't speak Polish, I never had a conversation with any one of them. I wish I had, because they came from the "old country," and I know nothing about what their lives were like before they came to America. I don't even know if they arrived by way of Ellis Island.

The communication I remember most is when my mother's mother, Victoria, pinched her grandchildren's cheeks, including mine, while she called me Davush. Pinching someone's cheek, as everyone knows, is the international symbol for love. Red cheeks were sure evidence that my grandmother loved you.

When I was a youngster, I looked around at my life and found that I was surrounded by things that I had no interest in. I also found that a lot of what I saw didn't make sense. I attended a Polish school, but my father didn't want me to learn how to speak Polish, either because he didn't want my brother and me to understand what he and my mother were saying or because he thought my English would suffer. Mass in Polish was just about as ridiculous to me as mass in Latin. I didn't understand either one. And I certainly did not want to spend my leisure time enjoying the major pastime of the men in the neighborhood, which was collecting pigeons, or as the French call them, *rats with wings*. Include me out.

I knew that I fell short of what was expected of me as a Catholic, a student, a neighbor, and a son. I was about as ordinary as a person could get. Nothing about me was outstanding and that was fine with me, but it didn't seem to be fine with the rest of the world. My grades told me I should be smarter, my parents told me I should be more responsible, and my religion told me I was a worm of the dust. I grew up thinking that surely one day my real parents, who were undoubtedly English Royalty, would make themselves known to me, and we would all retire to the drawing room for tea and polite conversation. Never happened. Instead, I would develop into a mediocre student, mediocre soldier, and later a mediocre entertainer. I grew into being a mediocre human being, in my own mind, and all because I unconsciously identified with my background and everything that was middle-of-the-road. Nobody expected much of me, I didn't expect much of myself, and so I lived a rather unremarkable life.

My heroes? Actually, I didn't have any, though I thought that Roy Rogers and Bernadette of Lourdes were pretty neat—Roy Rogers for his handsome face and Bernadette because she was so good that Jesus' mother appeared to her in a grotto. Like all Catholic children, I hoped that God, Jesus, Mary, or anybody would appear to me just once, anywhere. Never happened. And like most adolescent boys, I hoped that a handsome face was lurking behind all my pimples. Oh well.

The only thing I was interested in was reading comic books and eating Oreo cookies with milk. It is said that children find themselves in comic books and that's why boys usually like Superman. They are drawn to the idea of power. I wonder what I was drawn to by liking Little Lulu, Donald Duck, and his nephews Huey, Dewey, and Louie.

I'd like to say that, underneath it all, I was a seeker, longing to find what was sacred in the world. I'd like to say that, but I can't. I was never a seeker and sacredness was just not a part of my life. I assumed that what I had and what I was, wasn't much, but it was all that I could expect out of life, so I became satisfied with things as they were. There were lots of things I liked to do and a lot of things I hoped would happen. I just didn't go after much, because I didn't think I had what it took to pull it off. I took whatever came along and tried to make the best of it. Sometimes I did and sometimes I didn't.

Was there an epiphany that changed everything? Again, I'd like to say that there was an epiphany, and that it was incredibly dramatic so I could inspire you to great heights by telling you a spectacular story, but I can't. There was no epiphany, only the slow evolution of an average mind and if I inspire you in any way, it will be by reminding you of something that deep down you already know.

I now believe that my average mind is pretty spectacular and that every mind is pretty spectacular.

Every person can accomplish what they set out to do —if they just set out to do it by first accepting their enough-ness.

I also believe that no one is subject to their nationality, their skin color, or the way they were brought up, unless they consciously or unconsciously want to be because it serves some purpose.

I don't have to take whatever comes along; instead I can cause my life to be what I want it to be. I have also discovered that what other people expect of me isn't as important as what I expect of myself.

But most of all, I have discovered that I am enough just the way I am. If I never accomplish anything, and no one ever appears to me in a grotto or tells me that I'm as handsome as Roy Rogers, I'm enough just the way I am ... and from this great realization I can shape the rest of my life. I hope this book will help you to come to some of the same conclusions.

This book is about remembering who *you* are.

WHAT'S IMPORTANT
ABOUT WHO YOU ARE

THERE ARE MORE SELF-HELP BOOKS BEING SOLD in the world than ever before. These books pursue everything from personal transformation to how to get what you want from a world that doesn't want to give it to you. The sale of these books is a good sign, because it means that more and more people are taking an active role in the development of what they want their lives to look like, instead of just taking whatever comes along and making the best of it. What we must remember is:

> The thing in us that can make our life look the way we want, is more important than the changes we are able to make.

If we don't make what we *are* more important than what we *do*, we will live a lifetime of self-inflicted pressure to perform. The result of this way of living means we not only feel good about ourselves when we are accomplishing something, but we also feel bad about ourselves when we aren't.

Not a great way to go through life.

CONSTRUCTIVE SELF-TALK:

What I am is more important than what I do.

THE GREATEST NEED

BEYOND FOOD AND SHELTER, our greatest need as human beings is to matter. This need usually takes the form of wanting proof that in the midst of this great big world, we've got what it takes—that we are enough.

Long ago, I became absorbed by what I thought was life's most important issue: An acknowledgment of the cause-and-effect Spiritual system we live in. I have studied this system, used it myself, and taught others how to use this system to make their lives better. Along the way, however, I realized a very important thing. Even though we can use the cause-and-effect system to our own advantage, if we're not careful, we get to thinking that we are worthwhile only when we are doing so.

What we often overlook is the fact that the thing that uses the law of cause and effect is complete, regardless of what it causes or doesn't cause.

Every attempt to make your life better is important, but there is something that you need to fully understand first and foremost–you.

Whether you accomplish or don't accomplish anything during your entire lifetime, your existence is what makes you matter.

This simple Truth is probably the most important thing to know about ourselves: what we are creating isn't as important as who we get to be while we are creating.

CONSTRUCTIVE SELF TALK:

I matter because I exist.
I don't have to prove anything to anyone.

WHO AM I ANYWAY?

I'M NOT MY RÉSUMÉ, AND NEITHER ARE YOU. The most important question we can ask is: Who am I? Let's answer this question by first clarifying who we are *not*.

We are NOT:

> *our bodies*
>
> *our thoughts*
>
> *our feelings*
>
> *our careers*
>
> *our reviews*
>
> *our money*
>
> *our relationships*
>
> *our accomplishments*
>
> *our experience of life*

We are none of these things. We are that which

is *aware* of all these things. We are mind. We are not what we see in the mirror. We are that which is doing the seeing. We are mind. And the mind that we are, is complete, because it is some part of the sacredness of Life.

When you put your focus on this simple truth, you have creative freedom. This doesn't mean that your accomplishments are of no consequence. They are as important as you make them, but the key to a happy life is to always make yourself more important than what you do. You are always greater than what you think, what you know, what you have, and what you do. That's why, no matter what happens in your life, you are always in a position to start again and create something new.

Acknowledge your accomplishments, even praise yourself for having made them, but always leave a small place in your mind where your soul can whisper the following self-talk.

Constructive Self-Talk:

I am enough. I am more important than anything I will ever accomplish, for I am the sacred presence of life. It is with my enough-ness that I now cause my life to look the way I want it to look.

DISCOVERING
THE SACRED

"Nothing is at last sacred but the
integrity of our own mind."

– RALPH WALDO EMERSON

THE WORD SACRED HAS LONG BEEN GIVEN to that which is of God. I use the word in the same way, not to describe a God up in the skies that punishes and rewards, but rather a Life Force that exists within every person. You are sacred because the Life Force is within you.

Even though the most sacred thing *in* life ... *is* life ... in all of its shapes and forms, there is something unique in humans. When we look closely at human life, we find that humans are the only form of life that can appreciate sacredness. This is because human beings–all human beings–*are* sacred, not because of what they have accomplished or can accomplish, but because they exist.

Some people make sacredness a moral issue. They believe that the most important thing in life is to know the difference between right and wrong, good and bad, and then live accordingly. This idea is good as far as it goes, but it doesn't go far enough. Surely, there must be something more to being sacred than dancing between what is good and what is not. Being sacred is an unconditional quality of human life. We can't make ourselves sacred, and we can't keep ourselves from being sacred. We can only become aware that we *are* sacred.

The motto of the American Indian Church is: Everything Is Sacred. You'll notice there is no qualifier added to this statement. It doesn't say, everything that has been blessed by Indian elders is sacred, or everyone who has worked on behalf of world peace is sacred, or even everyone who has upheld the traditions of the American Indian is sacred. *Everything* is sacred. Period.

To get in touch with our sacredness we need to dispel the myth that someone can bestow sacredness upon us or that we can do something to become sacred, more sacred, more spiritual, more worthy, or more important to the Universe than we already are.

I believe this book will lead to the expansion of your awareness, and by writing it I hope to reveal the unconditional sacredness of life ... your life ... right now ... just as it is.

We are *as* spiritual, *as* perfect, *as* worthwhile and *as sacred* as we will ever be, and the only thing that we can ever become more of–is *aware*.

Constructive Self-Talk:

My mind is sacred because the Power that gave me life is still within me.

THE SHIFT IN CONSCIOUSNESS

THE EVOLUTION OF HUMAN CONSCIOUSNESS has brought humanity to the point where it is challenging beliefs that it has cherished for hundreds of years. Though these beliefs run far and wide, probably the most important one is what people believe about themselves and their relationship to God. Being a God-fearing person, for instance, no longer makes sense, and neither does believing in a God that punishes some and rewards others. This is *the God that never was*, but nonetheless a God that most of us believed in—a "sky God" that was decidedly separate from us.

We have also evolved beyond believing that human beings are intrinsically flawed. This view of life was undoubtedly fostered by those who wanted to manipulate others into believing they were flawed, so they could offer a way to get unflawed.

You are not now, nor have you ever been, flawed. The only thing that might be flawed is your perception of yourself, or your perception of what it means to be sacred, spiritual, or even human.

More than ever, it seems, people are not willing to drag the "dead corpse" of outworn beliefs into the future, or believe that something is true just because their parents believed it.

We have evolved to the point where we are ready to acknowledge our own views as valid, and if there isn't a religion or philosophy that supports those views, fine. Emerson wrote, "Trust thyself: every heart vibrates to that iron string." Trust that if you think something is right, if it doesn't hurt you or anyone else, it can be pursued as valid.

People are even starting to become comfortable saying they have no religion. Many of these people identify themselves as spiritual but not religious. This is not an indictment against religion, but rather a celebration of something that is bigger than all religions put together: the human Spirit.

Every religion attempts to define God and the relationship that human beings have with God and this makes perfect sense, because we try to understand everything. What we must remember is that God could not possibly be bound by the doctrine of any religion; for though God fills all time and space, God transcends all time and space.

Is there a difference between being religious and being spiritual? Yes. A religious person is one who agrees with and therefore adheres to the doctrine and traditions of a particular religion. A spiritual person is simply someone who exists. This distinction identifies the spiritual person as one who doesn't have to do anything or even believe in anything to be spiritual, whereas the religious person does.

It may disappoint some people to say it, but the truth is that ordinary human beings, regardless of religious affiliation, or even if they have no religious affiliation at all; regardless of what is believed or not believed: everyone is as spiritual as it is possible to be, because spirituality is not conditional. It comes with the territory of living. To be spiritual is to be alive, to simply exist. To be spiritual is not predicated on "good works" or staying within the prescribed parameters set by anyone. Again ... to be spiritual is to be alive!

Growing up, however, I had a very different image of what it meant to be spiritual and it certainly wasn't something that included me or anyone I knew. My image of a spiritual person was defined in lofty terms that go beyond being an average human being. The high-end of being spiritual was sainthood and the low-end was being saint-like. This menu of spirituality most probably came from stories of the saints I heard as a child. Saints had auras and halos, they fought dragons, wielded swords, burned in fires, or were the meek who would inherit the earth.

The most important ingredient for being a spiritual person was being willing to die for one's faith. Why was this important? Because that's what Jesus did, and my religion told me that if Jesus did it, I should be willing to do it too.

We are not more spiritual because we are religious, and nothing we can do, or not do, can make us less spiritual. No matter what happens in our lives, good or not, no matter how enlightened we become or don't become, we are spiritual beings on a self-created pathway of our unfolding understanding, and every step of the way we are as spiritual as we will ever become.

The shift in consciousness that is going on today means that people everywhere are starting to accept themselves without reservation, just as they are. Rather than asking ourselves what we are willing to die for, we must ask ourselves what are we willing to live for.

What a great way to live ... the way life was meant to be lived.

CONSTRUCTIVE SELF-TALK:

My life means what I say it means.
I decide what I shall believe and
leave others alone to think for themselves.

YOU ARE ENOUGH

IF AN ACTOR IS REVIEWED AS BEING ADEQUATE in a role, that actor is probably not flattered, because to most people being adequate is being just barely sufficient. The word *adequate*, however, actually means *being equal to the need*.

We all want to feel that we have what it takes to get along in life. We want to feel that we are equal to our aspirations and that if we want something, it may take a little work but we can get it if we try. We all want to feel adequate. This need is natural and the reason we have it is that at some deep level we know we are adequate. We know we are not only equal to but *bigger* than our aspirations, which means at some level we know we are enough. The challenge is to bring this feeling of enough-ness out into the open, so we can use it as a tool to make life better.

The driving force, then, behind much of what we do is the need to feel good about who we are, or what I am calling *the need to experience being enough*, and we will do just about anything to fulfill this need. We will say things we don't mean, do things we don't really want to do, and buy things that serve little purpose other than contribute to that vast network of illusions that promises to make us feel like we're enough. Some people even turn to drugs or alcohol because both give the illusion of enoughness, for a while at least.

We can use any of these things to make us feel like we're enough, but the feeling won't last for very long because there is something within us that knows better. Something that tugs at our ear and whispers, *Stop trying to become enough. You're already enough. You're enough because you exist, and you know it!*

The much-quoted statement of Marianne Williamson attests to this truth. "Our deepest fear is not that we are inadequate. Our deepest fear is that we are powerful beyond measure."

No matter what is going on in your life this very moment, you are adequate unto every need. You are enough, and your enough-ness is the launching pad from which you can cause your life to look the way you want it to look, if you let it.

What we don't realize is that every attempt to make ourselves feel like we're enough by adding something *to* our lives, moves us farther away from accepting that we are enough *now*. Even striving to become more successful, a worthy undertaking, can put the realization of *being enough* in jeopardy, if we're doing it to become worthwhile individuals.

You're not worthwhile because you have fulfilled your dreams. You are worthwhile because you exist. You're not enough because you have a good job. You're enough even if you haven't worked in thirteen years. You're not enough because you are loved by many people. You're enough even if nobody knows your name. You're not enough because your financial portfolio is enviable. You are enough even if you're dead broke. And becoming more successful doesn't make you enough, either. It only changes your experience. It doesn't change *you*.

Some time ago, I met a man who identified himself as "illegitimate" because his mother and father were not married when he was born. "How can life be illegitimate?" I asked him. Maybe in the eyes of a government or some religion, but certainly not in the eyes of someone who knows that life is bigger than all the governments and religions of the world. Paperwork doesn't validate anyone's existence. Existence validates itself.

You're enough because you exist, and it's that simple. And it is out of your enough-ness that can get a new job, experience love and success, and build a financial portfolio that satisfies you. Enough-ness is the tool. I'll show you how to use it later.

CONSTRUCTIVE SELF-TALK:

I don't need to become a worthwhile person, because I already am. No one and nothing can change the simple truth that I am enough just the way I am.

YOUR ENOUGH-NESS
IS TRANSCENDENT

LET'S TAKE A CLOSER LOOK AT THE SUBTLE THINGS that identify us. Human beings identity themselves by sex, name, Social Security number, nationality, skin color, sexual preference, or what they do for a living. Humans also identify themselves as married or single, Republican or Democrat. The list is endless. These things may describe something *about* us, but none of them describes what we *are*.

When we were young, we wanted our identity to match everyone else's, sort of like Woody Allen's character Zelig. Leonard Zelig took on the identity of the person he was with, because he needed to be liked. When we were young, we didn't want to stand out. We wanted to fit in. We wanted to be liked. Then we matured and we wanted our identity to be unique, *not* like everyone else's.

I can remember going to Toledo University as a freshman, feeling so inadequate. I put on my chinos, white button-down shirt, and crew-neck sweater. It didn't matter to me that most of the other guys were wearing this too; in fact that's what allowed me to walk the halls of TU feeling pretty good about myself. I looked like everyone else. I didn't stand out. In my own mind, I was a college student because I looked like one. Well, I soon realized that it took more than looking like a college student to be one. It took studying, and that's something I wasn't interested in. Four months later, I left college and joined the Air Force and spent the following four years looking like every other Zelig on Andrews Air Force Base. At this point in my life I obviously wanted to fit in, not realizing my true self yet. Go figure.

You are more than the color of your skin, your nationality, your marital status or what you do for a living.

You are Life—and life is bigger than the way it expresses itself. This means what you *are* transcends the way you are living as a human being, what you have accomplished and what you intend to accomplish. What you are transcends everything you've ever thought, said or done, and all of the experiences you've ever had, good or bad. You are life ... and that's the source of real enough-ness.

The entire realm of the transcendent is an interesting one. It has fascinated people for thousands of years and will undoubtedly continue to do so for thousands more, because it offers the human mind an opportunity to identify with something bigger than what it normally considers possible. The difference here is, we're reaching for something that is bigger than what we normally consider ourselves to *be*. Something that transcends all human experience. Where will we find it? Within our own awareness, but we have to look for it.

We have to look for something in us that is not seeking approval, that doesn't need support or agreement from anyone, something that doesn't get a sense of self-worth from the clothes it wears or the car it drives, something that feels separate from the world of experience, opinion, and judgment. Something transcendent.

Religions are based on this transcendent phenomenon. Most religions however, separate the transcendent from the human being as something to be worshiped from afar rather than recognized as an already accomplished reality about the self.

Jesus knew that a person's identity was not a religious issue, it was a spiritual issue that extended beyond all religions. He proved this by saying, "Now

31

you are sons and daughters of the most high" and even went on to tell us that greater things than he did, would we do. He was *not* saying, "I am enough. You, however, are chopped liver." Perhaps some of you may remember Jackie Gleason, as an angry Ralph Kramden, saying to his wife, played by Audrey Meadows, "I am king of this household and you are nothing." To this she replied, "Great, king over nothing."

It's pretty clear that Ralph Kramden needed to be in charge of his wife to feel good about himself. It was Ralph's kingdom and he was King. To me, Jesus was saying, the Kingdom of God is within all people, and because this is true, all people are enough whether they realize it or not. This means that an individual doesn't have to accept or agree with any of what are considered to be Christian or Judaic values to be enough. Atheists are enough!

Ah, religion! Were you taught that the most spiritual family was a God- fearing family? If you were, then you, like many other people, tried to love and fear God at the same time, hoping that if you learned how to do this, you would obtain God's favor and avoid God's wrath, and become in God's eyes ... enough.

The Upanishads reveal something liberating in reference to seeking God's approval: "Thou, God, seest me perfect." (Or we could say, Life, thou seest me perfect.) This simply means that I don't have to seek God's approval, because God's love is unconditional. In God's eyes I am enough, and I'll always be enough, because God isn't a person. God is the Creative Power of Life that has placed Itself within everything and everyone. I am always complete *in* and *to* that power and if I weren't, I wouldn't exist.

It is understandable why religions separated the transcendent from man. The argument must have certainly been something like, *If something transcends human life, it must be separate from human life.* This line of reasoning does not take into account the obvious: human beings are life, and if life is bigger than the way it is being expressed, then human beings are transcendent by nature. Human beings are greater than the way they have expressed or experienced life.

When we identify ourselves as transcendent life, we are able to put things in right perspective and in so doing to live our lives empowered by our own identity, rather than looking outside of ourselves for someone or something to forgive us, save us, approve of us, or make our lives better. We stop looking *for* the transcendent because we realize we are the transcendent. Our salvation lies in the knowledge that "what you are looking for, you are looking with."

This means that human beings have within themselves something that transcends every conceivable consideration, something powerful, something creative, something spectacularly wonderful! Metaphysicians call this something God, Spirit, or Divine Mind. Some call it the Christ Mind. I call it Life. But what we call it isn't important. All that matters is that we acknowledge this part of our nature and learn how to use it to make our lives better.

The eternal quest then, whether we realize it or not, is not for God or the Holy Grail. It's for the transcendent Self ... and when we discover this transcendent self, we will realize we have discovered what religions have been calling God for thousands of years. No greater discovery could be made. Think of it—when you go to that place within your own mind that feels complete, you have entered the Kingdom. You have found God. God is completeness.

Before you attempt to do anything, seek first the Kingdom of Enough. And if you don't like Bible references, make up something that amounts to the same thing. You might affirm the following:

❈

CONSTRUCTIVE SELF-TALK:

My experience of life does not define me, for my identity can only be found in that place within my own mind that transcends my experience. Before I do anything I remind myself that I am complete, and it is from and with my completeness that I proceed.

WHEN YOU KNOW
YOU'RE ENOUGH

WHEN YOU KNOW YOU'RE ENOUGH, you meet life feeling good about yourself just the way you are, without having to make excuses for what you haven't accomplished, or becoming all puffed up because of what you have. Enough-ness seems to create a sense of equilibrium. The person who accepts the self as enough doesn't need to be praised and doesn't fall apart because he or she is criticized. These people remember that both praise and criticism are just someone's opinion.

Artist Georgia O'Keeffe writes:

I get out my work and have a show for myself before I have it publicly. I make up my own mind about it—how good or bad or indifferent it is. After that, the critics can write what they please. I have already settled it for myself, so flattery and criticism go down the same drain and I am quite free.

When you know you're enough just the way you are, your relationship to yourself is healthy and your energy is spent creating the kind of life that you want, not to feel better about who you are but to experience your creative ability. You need to experience your creativity without the burden of having the end result mean something spectacular or make you feel like you're somebody.

When you know you're enough, you're comfortable with your skin color, your background, your nationality, and your talents and abilities, because you know that none of these things define you. They only define something about your body, your experience, or something you've done. They do not, however, define *you*, for you are none of these things.

When you know you are enough, you don't waste time trying to impress people, because you know that the way people think about you is secondary to the way you think about yourself. When you know you are enough, you are sure that you can accomplish what you set out to do, because the source of your enough-ness is life, and life is always enough.

Does the Bible say anything about being enough? When Jesus tells us that the Kingdom of Heaven is not only within, but within *now*, he is saying, there is a transcendent place within you that has never been made more by what you've done and never made less by what you didn't do. This is the place where you are enough and the place Jesus refers to when he says, "Which of you, by taking thought, can add one cubit to his stature?" Nothing we can think, say, or do, can add to or subtract from what we intrinsically are.

Is there any scientific proof that wherever life appears, it is always enough?

Maybe the hologram tells part of the story. The hologram is a three-dimensional image of an object, produced by recording the patterns of interference that occur when a split laser beam illuminates a photographic plate or film. The interesting thing about a hologram is that if a piece of the picture image is cut from the whole, that piece contains the entire picture. Similarly, each of us is a part of the Source from which we came, and each of us contains or represents that Source in its entirety. This is not a religious issue. It is a *life* issue that some religions think of as a spiritual truth. Regardless of what we want to call this source, we are inextricably one with its nature.

The hologram is enough because it contains everything that makes it a hologram, and a piece of the hologram is also enough because it always represents the whole. You are enough because you contain everything that makes you a thinking center of Life's Creative Intelligence. This means you are enough because you exist.

To some people mere existence, however, is not a credential for enough-ness. This way of thinking is passed on from generation to generation and creates an army of people who feel that they are defective in some way. These people live their lives "in quiet desperation," usually as people-pleasers, and can be manipulated very easily, because they hunger for anything that makes them feel good about themselves. It's the "Tell me that what I've done is wonderful, or what I know is wonderful, and I'll follow you anywhere" syndrome.

And don't confuse loving what you *do* with loving what you *are*. They are two separate issues. We spend a lifetime doing, so it's no wonder that we want what we do to amount to something. It does. What you do amounts to whatever you say it amounts to, and also whatever it might amount to, in the collective mind we all share, but what you *do* can never compete with what you *are*.

It may be hard at first to feel good about ourselves just because we exist, but it's the only thing that will ever satisfy the soul—and we know it.

❈

CONSTRUCTIVE SELF-TALK:

I know that I am enough. There may be religions and philosophies that agree with me, but that's not why I am enough. I am enough because I was born to express life, and life is always enough.

WHEN YOU DON'T KNOW YOU'RE ENOUGH

WHEN WE DON'T KNOW WE'RE ENOUGH we waste most of our time trying to prove ourselves. Another way of saying it is that when we don't know we're enough, we waste most of our time trying to *become* enough. Everything becomes a test to prove that we are either equal to everyone else or better than everyone else, and usually we want to prove that we're better. Why? Because when not being enough becomes a way of life, it takes more than being enough to compensate; it takes believing we are *better* than everyone else. When the pendulum swings in one direction, it then swings back in the opposite direction just as far.

I would guess that people who need to think of themselves as better than anyone else are people who secretly believe they are less.

Those who are the most needy for attention and

approval are the ones who have spent the most time feeling inadequate. This inadequate feeling often shows up as a superiority complex. Most psychologists believe, however, that there is no such thing as a superiority complex. The only person who feels superior is one who is covering up a feeling of inferiority.

People who come to the kitchen table or the boardroom table trying to *prove* that they are worth something always bring negative baggage with them. They equate being enough with their ability to influence. If they get their way, they feel good about themselves–mission accomplished. If they don't get their way, they don't feel good about themselves–mission aborted. In other words, the person who feels incomplete will almost always have the same mission: to create something that enables them to feel complete.

This state of mind also affects groups. It's very hard for a group of people to deal intelligently with an idea when one or more of the people in the group have a desperate need for recognition in some form. Someone once said, "There are no limits to how far we can go if no one cares who gets the credit."

People who live life trying to prove something rather than be something, hate to be wrong, shame easily and seldom feel really good about themselves. This is no way to go through life. I know, because I've done it and the results are devastating. During my I'm-not-enough years, no matter what I was doing, it wasn't good enough. *It* wasn't good enough, because *I* wasn't good enough. And when someone had a negative opinion of me, though I would defend myself, I would privately agree, because unconsciously I needed to be treated in a way that matched my self-image.

This tendency comes from a habit of identifying with the outside rather than with what's inside. This is a common mistake that people make when they allow what they have or have not accomplished to identify them.

I once heard a mother identify herself as the one who was responsible for her son's triumphs. When she spoke about her son, it was clear that her self-worth was wrapped up in raising such a wonderful son. Should she give herself any credit? Of course. But what if she never had a son? Would she be worth less? Of course not! The point is, we are bigger than, more important than—yes, worth more than—all of our accomplishments put together. And if we never accomplish anything, we will still be worth the price of admission to this life.

Youngsters make the same mistake when they join a group, thinking that this newfound affiliation will somehow make them "somebody." Joining a group, any group, doesn't necessarily mean that a person lacks self-worth. The question is, why does anyone belong to a group?

If we join a group because we want to celebrate our enough-ness with people of like mind and similar interests, it is the act of a healthy-minded person. If we're joining a group to *become* enough, it's the act of a person who feels inadequate just being themselves.

Parents, or the adults in a child's life, ought to be the major supporter of the child's enough-ness. This can be done by being examples of enough-ness and also by eliminating the tendency to fawn over the child when the child has accomplished something. Recognition is fine, but in the extreme, it often suggests (to the child) that the child's worth depends on what they have *done* rather than on what they *are*. Sure, recognition will make children feel good for a while, but if it is excessive, it can also contribute to a belief that the only reason they are worthwhile is because of what they do.

The first thing every child looks for when he or she arrives here on this planet is confirmation that they are wanted just as they are. The mindful parent finds a way to make what the child is, more important than what the child does. And it's not that what the child does is unimportant. It's that compared to what the child is, it is less important.

How do you know if you're acting mindfully as a parent? Ask yourself if you like your child more when he or she plays better on the soccer field or the football field, or gets better grades. You may like his or her performance more, but do you actually like the child more? And if you respond to this question by saying, "I can't separate the child from the performance," you're headed for disaster. At some conscious or unconscious level children will know that they have your genuine approval only when they are pleasing you. This state of mind will lead you to liking your child when your expectations are met, and not liking your child when your expectations are not met. Your child will not only know but feel the difference. Why? Because your child knows what you really love and, like you, wants to be loved for what he or she is not for what he or she does. This is why some children rebel. Indeed, this is why we rebel.

The best gift you can give a child is the unquestionable approval of his or her existence. Sound simple? Try it. It may the hardest thing you've ever done, but it's the most important!

What must be noticed here is that if parents don't think that they themselves are enough, they will unconsciously pass this way of living on to their children.

It's no wonder we have a society that succumbs to anything that promises to eliminate its feeling of inadequacy. We will buy, rent, or borrow, even visit places that promise to make us feel like we are important, at least for a while.

CONSTRUCTIVE SELF-TALK:

*From now on, my assessment of myself
is not predicated on any experience I've ever had
or the way anyone has ever treated me.*

*In fact, I am not even subject to the way
I have treated myself.*

*I come to the table of life feeling good
about being exactly who I am.*

THE VICTIM

ANOTHER ROLE THAT THE PERSON WHO DOESN'T feel complete takes on is that of the victim. It's an unflattering role but one that has a payoff. It attracts attention as well as sympathy—two things that create the illusion of enough-ness. The illusion, however, never really satisfies and the victim knows it.

Why, then, doesn't the victim stop playing the role? Because though the payoff is not a positive one, at least it's a payoff. It reminds the individual that they are alive, or at least that they can command attention. The idea that negative attention is better than no attention at all, has long been known.

The person experiencing the payoff of victimhood either doesn't know how to stop being a victim or has spoken the script of victimhood for so long that they believe it themselves.

The best way to break the habit of victimhood is

to see the "self" as enough. We don't need anyone's attention or approval if we are enough. The problem is, we don't approve of ourselves because we have given more attention to our faults than we have given to our enough-ness.

Am I saying we don't have faults? Of course not. I'm saying that our faults, our mistakes, and even our weaknesses don't define us. They only define choices we have consciously or unconsciously made along the way.

You are not the choices you've made. You are the chooser. And the chooser can always choose again, and again and again. Attached to every choice, of course, there is a consequence, but the "self" never changes. The only thing that can change is our experience.

We are the "thing" that allows itself to feel weak, make mistakes, create faults, but we are separate from all three. We transcend all three. We are a mind that can choose the way it's going to identify itself: at the level of what it has chosen or at the level of what it is.

We can choose to relate to life in strength or weakness. Neither defines us, for what we are is not only bigger than the experiences we can create but bigger than the identity we come up with. It's not until we realize that we are one with the Creative Power of the Universe that we enter the realm of understanding our real identity—a sacred identity. The person who is conscious of being sacred can never be a victim.

CONSTRUCTIVE SELF-TALK:

I don't need anyone's attention but my own, and I have it. I refuse to be a victim for any reason, because I am in control of the way I respond to everything and everyone.

THE MOST
SATISFYING PATH

UNDOUBTEDLY, THE CATALYST BEHIND many successes in the world is a need to prove something because one feels inadequate, but the best path, the path that satisfies the soul, is one of completeness every step of the way. Taking this path makes living a joy, because it doesn't postpone that feeling of being enough. Being enough is not something we achieve. It's something we are.

The most satisfying path, then, isn't so much what we are accomplishing, but rather how we grow while we are accomplishing.

We get to be the creative power of the Universe, conscious of itself. We get to be whole, complete, enough!

The purpose of life is to satisfy the soul, and though acknowledging your accomplishments can help in this effort, it cannot take you the full distance. The only thing that can satisfy your soul is an answer to the question, who am I? You are an individualized expression of Life, of greater consequence and magnitude than anything you will ever accomplish.

When we focus on the fact that we are enough *now*, the beginning, the middle and the end of every journey—whether it's finding a mate or getting a better job—is filled with a sense of well-being. We may complete an experience and even be thrilled by the outcome, but we know that we are no more complete than when we started out.

You see, we are either enough right now or we're not; and if we are, then we're challenged *by* our enough-ness to live that way.

The problem is, most of us don't listen to the inner voice that says, "You're enough because you exist." We ignore it because being enough doesn't fit the image we have of ourselves. We have spent so much time thinking of ourselves as not being enough that enough-ness seems very far away. We may have a sense of being surrounded by the Life Force, but we forget that the Life Force is also within us. And if the Life Force is *within* us, we are enough.

How easy it is to be Bible-oriented and still gloss over one of its most important statements, "Man was made in the image and likeness of [the Life Force we call] God." And if the Life Force is enough, *we* must be enough.

Being made in the image and likeness of God isn't something we have to strive for. It's something we must have the courage to accept.

The root of all of our problems, then, is a faulty self-image, because the natural tendency of mind is to surround itself with whatever it has embodied. If I embody fear and doubt, I will surround myself, to one degree or another, with people and circumstances that reflect fear and doubt. If, however, I embody faith and trust, I will surround myself with people and circumstances that reflect faith and trust. The key word here is embody.

Constructive Self-Talk:

I satisfy my soul by remembering that who I am is more important than anything I will ever accomplish.

EMBODIMENT

By "embody" I don't mean just giving some *attention to*. I mean being the *personification* of a particular idea. The original meaning of the word *embody* was to give a body to, as in giving a body to an incarnating Spirit. If I embody the idea of prosperity, for instance, I am giving prosperity a body, a place in my mind and life. If, however, I embody the idea of lack, I am giving lack a body, a place in my mind and my experience. The obvious way to proceed is to embody only what you wish to experience.

Probably the simplest way to understand the way I am using the word embody can be found when someone wants you to realize that you are always playing the role of the martyr. They will say, "You're such a martyr; in fact next to the word *martyr* in the dictionary is your picture."

We all have a personal mental dictionary that defines every word we're aware of. Some of our definitions are correct, in that they reflect the commonly accepted way of defining that word, and some are not. For instance, I used to think that the word *squander* meant to horde money. I was wrong. It means exactly the opposite. *Squander* means to waste or throw money away.

It might be interesting to think of God as having a personal dictionary too. And behind every positive adjective, God has placed the picture of everyone who has ever lived. But we don't get to experience what's in God's dictionary, only what's in our own, for such is the nature of life. Regardless of what God wants for us, we get to experience only what we have embodied.

If you were to look up the word *successful* in the dictionary of your own mind, would you find your picture? If it's not there, it's because you have an incomplete definition of success. You haven't included yourself. You haven't put your picture next to a quality of life that you were created to experience. Why is it up to you to put your own picture in that dictionary? Because it's *your* dictionary; it's the way you define the word, and you put *into* the dictionary of your own mind whatever you consciously or unconsciously identify with.

Maybe you haven't exactly put your picture next

to the word *failure*, but it might appear next to the word *disappointment*. Why would we do that? Because that's the way we see the part we play in life. We see ourselves as always disappointing someone. If not our parents or our significant other, if not the company we work for, then ourselves. Well, maybe we have disappointed many people. So what. That was then, and this is now. Just remember, you're the one who puts your picture where you want it to be. If you want your picture to be next to the word success in your own mental dictionary, put it there; and start thinking of yourself as a success regardless of where else in the dictionary your picture used to appear. It's the way you think about yourself *now* that counts.

Maybe you're focused on the fact that your picture doesn't appear under the word *success* in your parents' mental dictionary. So what. It's what is in the dictionary of *your* mind that makes a difference, not what is in your parents' mind, or your mate's mind, or your boss's mind.

Make sure that your self-image is based on values that are constructive and life-affirming, values that inspire not depress. And if you're going to adopt opinions, adopt your own, not someone else's, because the natural tendency of your mind is to surround yourself with a life that reflects whatever your image of yourself is. Make sure that what you are embodying is healthy-minded.

In some cultures, it is blasphemous for a man to rise above his father's place in society. It's considered a slap in the face. If you hold this to be true, you will unconsciously find a way to sabotage every advancement that comes your way. Either you will not get that really wonderful job or, if you do, you'll find a way to keep yourself at a certain level while those around you advance, and all because you have fashioned a self-image out of values that should have been destroyed long ago.

If you take a close look at your life, you'll find that you have embodied certain ideas to the exclusion of others. Maybe you've embodied strength or courage or honesty. How do you know if you've embodied these character qualities? No matter what's going on, you always exhibit them, regardless of the situation and whether or not they get noticed. You have made these qualities so much a part of your own self-image that you don't even think much about them. They are practically automatic responses to life. That's embodiment.

Can we embody *prosperity*? Yes, but many people think that prosperity is having money, and they won't put their picture next to the word prosperity in the mental dictionary of their own mind until they get a certain amount of money.

In his book *Spiritual Economics*, Dr. Eric Butterworth states, " Prosperity is a way of living and thinking, and not just money or things. Poverty is a way of living and thinking and not just a lack of money and things."

When it comes to money, money isn't what's important. What's important is the way we *think about* money. What does money represent?

Dr. Butterworth goes on to state, "Prosperity is Spiritual well-being." Let's use Dr. Butterworth's idea. If we want to end up with a self-image of being a prosperous person, we must embody an idea of prosperity that is separate from how much money we have and base our prosperous self-image on something that exists at the spiritual level. What is that something? Our identity *in* and *as* the Life Force. A Life Force that contains within itself an infinite supply of all that is good. And if this is true about the Life Force, it's true about us, but we must claim it as true. We must embody it.

If the Life-Force had a mental dictionary, your face would be next to every word that connotes the good life, including prosperity. And of course, so would everyone else's.

We are prosperous now, if only we would know it. Make this simple truth the way you live and think, and you'll find that prosperity has become an automatic response to life, consistently and naturally.

You are bigger than the image you have of yourself. Your self-image creates your experience. Your job is to embody the ideas that you decide are important.

CONSTRUCTIVE SELF-TALK:

I embody the ideas that I think are important.
I am prosperous now, and I know it, because I
have embodied the idea of prosperity.

HOW TO BEGIN: THE KINGDOM OF ENOUGH

THE NEXT TIME YOU CONFRONT SOMETHING you want to do, start by seeking first the *kingdom of enough*. Start by telling yourself that you are enough without it, and don't be afraid that this state of mind will eliminate wanting to do it. It won't. What it will do is to remind you that you are bigger than anything you are able to accomplish–bigger than your failures and, yes, bigger than your successes.

Train yourself to develop the consciousness of what you are seeking. In his book, *The Seven Habits of Highly Effective People*, Steven Covey tells us to "start with the end in mind." Good advice. Start with your enough-ness, and then identify the end result: what you want to happen. It might be peace of mind, prosperity, health, satisfying work, good relationships, or whatever.

Next, embody every nuance of the end result you have chosen. Then let the Law of Growth within you do the rest. It will give birth to the end result that you have so faithfully embodied.

John was raised in a family of "have nots" and so it seemed quite natural to John to be a "have not" himself. John was an individual who insisted on identifying himself as poor. He could identify only with what *was*, never with what *could be*. It was difficult for him to start with the end (in this case prosperity) in mind.

A friend of mine asked John to put on his best clothes, go downtown, and sit in the lobby of the finest hotel. John agreed. When he walked into the hotel he felt conspicuously out of place, but he found a chair and sat down anyway. As the day wore on, he got a little bored, so he bought a newspaper and started to read. There was a lot to read in the newspaper that day so John got quite absorbed in his paper. When he finally laid the paper aside, he looked up and realized that he felt a little more comfortable being in such luxurious surroundings.

The next morning John reported back to my friend, telling him that he didn't think it did much good. My friend told John to go back to the same hotel and do it again. Well, he did. When he walked in this time, the concierge nodded respectfully, having seen John the day before, saying, "Good morning, sir." "Good morning," replied John. John went right for the newsstand, bought a newspaper, sat down and started to read. After a while, John got hungry so he got up and asked the concierge if there was a coffee shop in the hotel. "We have a fine restaurant, just over there. I'm sure you will be pleased, sir." It wasn't long before John felt as comfortable eating in this hotel as he did reading the newspaper.

Suddenly John realized why my friend asked him to put himself in the middle of such opulence. My friend knew that John needed to become comfortable with what he wanted to experience, an idea that John has held to be sacred from that day to this.

If you want to experience something new, you must find a way to become comfortable with it. You must embody it.

You see, mind creates out of what it does to itself. No one knows exactly how mind does this, but it does. The founder of the Religious Science movement, Dr. Ernest S. Holmes, wrote a book titled, *The Science of Mind* in which he states, "Man, by thinking, can bring into his experience whatsoever he desires —if he thinks correctly, and becomes a living embodiment of his desires."

How do we become the living embodiment of a desire? If my desire is to be successful, I must mentally embody the idea of success in all of its nuances. I must think thoughts of success, acknowledge success wherever it appears, and let myself feel successful right now, because I am a complete manifestation of life's creative power. In addition to focusing on success, I must give no power to failure. What we focus on, we embody, and what we embody, we create.

Start with the idea that you are enough because you exist, and then build on that enough-ness until you reach the point where you have embodied the experience you are in the process of creating.

We're not trying to cause something to happen to make us feel like we're enough. Quite the opposite. We are using our enough-ness as the foundation upon which we satisfy our own creativity.

You are bigger than the experiences you are able to cause. Remember the premise of the book on page two? *Life is bigger than the philosophy, teaching, or religion that attempts to explain it. You are life.* We could also say: Life in you is bigger than the experience you are having, be it sickness, financial lack, loneliness, or unemployment, and because it's bigger, because it transcends the world of experience, you are in a position to change it. Your identity as an individualization of the creative power of the universe is what enables you to create the kind of life you desire.

Let's remember that what we do is never as important as what we are conscious of being, when we're doing it.

Constructive Self-Talk:

*I am comfortable with what
I have decided to experience.*

SELF-IMAGE

CONSCIOUSLY OR UNCONSCIOUSLY, we surround ourselves with circumstances and people that reflect our own self-image; and if something does not reflect the image we have of ourselves, we find ways to get rid of it. This is true of the positive and the negative.

Though we were created to personify completeness, our experience will be the result of what we image ourselves to be. Most of this imaging is unconscious.

People who identify with lack and limitation will surround themselves with people and circumstances that to them represent these negative qualities. And the opposite is also true. Individuals who identify with wealth and opulence surround themselves with whatever represents the same to them.

It's not a matter of the way we would *like* our lives to be. Everyone would like a wonderful life, but that does not mean it's going to happen. Why? Because we do not necessarily get to experience what we would like, or want, or deserve. We experience what we have embodied. We experience our image of ourselves.

This is great news for those of us who are willing to change our self-image and disheartening news for those who are not willing.

If our self-image is that of a poor struggling human being, we will make life a struggle. We will find that no matter what we're attempting to do, there is always a block of some kind, but the real block is our perception, in the way we are looking at something. Is the glass half empty or half full?

If we think of ourselves as unlovable, we are creating a self-fulfilling prophecy. We are pushing love away from us without realizing it. "But," you may say, "I have never been lucky in love." That's the problem! Love is not a matter of luck or being at the right place at the right time. It's a matter of the image we have embodied.

Your image attracts what is like it and repels what isn't. People who have a healthy self-image, whether that image is forged out of family values, a religion, or a particular brand of psychology, will appreciate life and, in the process, express love, and because they are *expressing* love, they will undoubtedly be loved in return.

If we lack a healthy self-image, we will attract either no one at all, a fixer-upper who wants to invest time and energy in changing us, or someone who, (like us), doesn't have a very healthy self-image. What a combination that makes. Two people who share the same distaste for life.

People who don't have a healthy self-image often feel vindicated when corroborating evidence proves that they are unloved, unwanted, and unappreciated. This is when the person says, "See, I'm right, nobody loves me."

The question is, do you want to be right, or do you want to love and be loved? If you want love in your life, change your self-image into a loving, giving person, regardless of who is or isn't in your life at this time. And let this new image you have of yourself guide the way you deal with everything and everyone. Embody the very qualities you want to attract in someone else.

Ralph Waldo Emerson tells us, "If you want a friend you must be a friend." If you want love you must embody and express love, *now*. If you want to live a prosperous life, embody the idea of prosperity and dare to express the consciousness of prosperity *now*.

If you want to experience being enough, you must accept that you are enough now, and dare to live that way. If you want love in your life, you must eliminate every idea that speaks of its absence and develop instead a consciousness that gives of itself to a world that is ready for it.

Years ago, a woman in one of my Self-Talk classes said, "I realized why I never had love in my life when I heard myself say, 'My mother used to tell me that I would never find anyone to love me.' Guess what?" my student said, "I haven't." This was not a self-fulfilling prophecy, it was a mother-fulfilling prophecy that came true because the daughter made her mother's opinion a part of her own. Today, this student is happily married, because she finally disagreed with her mother and now thinks for herself.

The best approach to shaping our lives is to first accept our enough-ness and then decide what we want to experience, be it health, happiness, love, or rewarding work. Next, we set out to embody the end result. This is called the development of consciousness. We can experience only what we have developed in our own minds.

The farmer starts by knowing that the soil needs to be fertile. It's enough. It has within it the essential ingredients necessary to grow the seed.

Next, the seed is planted. Then the farmer waters it appropriately, allowing the entire growth process to take place.

The soil I am talking about is the soil of your mind. You're going to plant an idea in your own mind, knowing that your mind is enough. It has within it everything necessary to grow your idea. Now it only needs watering. We "water" our idea by embodying every nuance of what the end result represents.

Here are four steps:

Know that your mind is enough.

Identify the end result of what you want.

Embody every nuance of what the end result represents.

Acknowledge the results of your work.

All four steps happen in your mind; therefore, your mind is all you need in order to create the kind of life you desire.

CONSTRUCTIVE SELF-TALK:

My self-image is healthy because it is based on what I already am.

THE STUFF WORKS

YOU'VE HEARD IT BEFORE, "STOP WAITING for your dreams to come true. Your dreams are waiting for *you* to come true." Regardless of what appears, we must claim what we *want* to appear as a *present reality* in our minds and trust that what is embodied in our minds must appear in our experience.

How this causes fulfillment, no one knows. All anyone knows it that this stuff works! Rev. Frederick Eikerenkotter (Rev. Ike), the master of Thinko-nomics says, "You can't lose with the stuff I use." He is, of course, referring to the power of mind.

Every human being has the ability to effect change, to influence life in some way. The baby laughs as it watches the ball it has thrown roll across the room and bump into a table. The adult enjoys watching the seed that was planted in fall become the flower that blooms in spring. We all have an affection for our ability to influence life.

The source of this ability must lie within our own minds; after all, what is it that decides to influence life? Mind. The way we think about something changes our experience and as I said, no one really knows why this is so, only that it is so.

The way we think about money, for instance, determines our experience of money. If we believe that money is the root of all evil, at some level we'll be pushing money away from us. Dr. Raymond Charles Barker tells us that "money is God in action," which means that the amount of money we have is the "inevitable consequence" of using the inner Life Force at the level of having that amount.

If we could see into the inner working of mind, we'd see that in the larger scheme of things, we don't get paid for what we do. We get paid for what we know. And if we don't get paid enough, it's often because we don't think that what we know is worth much.

If we walk through life always thinking that we are *not enough*, we will never have enough money, enough love, enough of anything.

The thing to remember is, since we have the *ability to influence life* (because we can think) we can influence the image we have of ourselves. We can change our self-image into a healthy one. We can also change an unhealthy image of money into a healthy one. But this change takes work. It takes a conscious commitment to upgrading what we let go on in our mind. We can change the way we react to everything and everyone, if we want to. Yes, this stuff works, but we've got to work it.

Dr. Victor Frankl was in concentration camps, including Auschwitz, between 1942 and 1945. During that time both of his parents, as well as other family members, were killed. Dr. Frankl knew that though someone could make his body a prisoner, they couldn't make a prisoner of his mind. To keep his mind healthy, he focused it on his wife. He writes, " My mind still clung to the image of my wife. A thought crossed my mind. I didn't even know if she were alive, and had no means of finding out (during all of my prison life there was no outgoing or incoming mail); but at that moment it ceased to matter. There was no need to know; nothing could touch the strength of my love and the thoughts of my love."

Dr. Frankl's statement celebrates the power of his own mind. He refused to be influenced by his surroundings.

In his much celebrated book *Man's Search for Meaning*, which has sold about nine million copies worldwide and has been translated into twenty-three languages, he writes, "There is nothing in the world, I venture to say, that would so effectively help one survive even the worst conditions as the knowledge that there is a meaning in one's life."

What is the meaning of your life? That is for you to answer, but I venture to say that nothing in the world would so effectively help you to survive even the worst conditions as the knowledge that you meet life as a complete being, and that your ability to influence life can never cease to be.

In some cases it may not be easy to exercise the authority of your own mind over conditions, but it is possible. After citing Dr. Victor Frankl's way of dealing with life, any suggestions I make might sound characterless. I will make them anyway.

If you're having a problem with someone at the office, don't have his or her picture next to the word *adversary* in your mental dictionary. Have it next to the word *friend*, or at least next to the words fellow *traveler*. The words we use to label someone usually cause us to relate to them in a particular way. Give everyone "harmless passage" through your mind.

Next, try not to argue people out of their ideas. They paid for them. Let them have them. You are only in charge of what you think. People who have conflicting ideas can get along if they respect each other. Don't wait to be respected. It's your turn. Offer a bit of respect to someone you disagree with and watch the relationship change for the better.

The point is, you either have the ability to influence your own life or you don't. Whatever you decide will be the foundation upon which you will build the rest of your life.

The Life Force that created you out of itself allows you to use its creative power, with one prerequisite, and that is: though you partake of its nature, you will only experience what dominates your mind. If lack and limitation dominate your thinking, lack and limitation will be your experience. The opposite is, of course, also true.

You can think thoughts that embody the idea of abundance and you can keep from thinking thoughts that embody lack, but you've got to know you can. Why not give it a try. Why not give the creative principle in your mind the opportunity to respond to thoughts of being a have, rather than a have-not?

❀

CONSTRUCTIVE SELF-TALK:

*Because my good is determined by the way
I use my mind, I will now use my mind
in the most constructive way I can
and let people think the way they want to.
I think what I ought to be thinking
and keep from thinking what works against me.*

WHO TOLD YOU, YOU WEREN'T ENOUGH?

THE BIBLE STORY OF ADAM AND EVE'S banishment from the garden of Eden serves a good purpose here. It is written that after being created, Adam and Eve knew they were naked and they were not ashamed. After eating the apple from the tree, they discovered both good and evil and were ashamed of their nakedness. God spoke to Adam and said, "Adam, where art thou?" Adam replied, "I heard thy voice in the garden, and I was afraid because I was naked." Now here's the usable line: God said, "Who told you, you were naked?

What does this story have to do with being enough? We were born complete, and somewhere along the line we started to think of ourselves as incomplete. Who told us we weren't enough? How did we get this idea? Was it passed on to us from the way our parents treated us, or was it something we assumed because of some physical disability, or disorder? Maybe we felt we weren't enough simply because of some indefinable thing about us. Or maybe we just went along with the idea that human beings are intrinsically flawed by nature.

No matter where it came from or how long we've had it, we must get rid of this feeling of incompleteness because it makes us approach life in a way that is unbecoming to our true identity.

Start to think of yourself as a person who is worthy of being loved and watch people start responding to you in a different way. This is because whether you are aware of it or not, you teach people how to treat you by means of the image you have of yourself. The mind that thinks of itself as complete, acts complete and treats people as if they were complete. This mind is very attractive. This mind is a loving mind and will certainly be loved in return.

You are worthy of being loved because you exist, but to attract love you must express love.

That's just the way life is. The thing to remember is that you can re-invent the way you think of yourself if you give yourself permission to do just that. Where once you listened to a voice that said or intimated that you weren't enough, now listen to your own voice telling you that you *are* enough. No memory, no physical, mental, or emotional disability can keep you from realizing your enough-ness.

Motivational speaker John Foppe was born without arms. He earned a Master's degree and was recognized by the U.S. Junior Chamber of Commerce as one of the "Ten Outstanding Young Americans." This prestigious award recognizes young leaders for their positive contributions to society. John says, "Our only real handicaps are those mental and emotional ones that prevent us from participating fully in life. How we feel and what we think clearly determines what we do. Simply put, our attitudes control our actions."

John didn't let his physical body determine what his life would be like. He knew that the way he felt and what he thought were more important than anything else and he proved it. He didn't prove it to *become* enough. He proved it, out of his enough-ness.

If we feel inadequate, we might as well *be* inadequate, because the way we think and feel about ourselves determines our experience of life. But the truth is, regardless of the image we have of ourselves, we are *not* inadequate, and allowing ourselves to think that we are is the only sin we will ever commit.

CONSTRUCTIVE SELF-TALK:

I am in charge of the way I feel about everything, including myself; and since I think about myself in a healthy-minded way, I feel good.

STOP WAITING: RE-INVENT NOW

MOST OF US HAVE BEEN TAUGHT that the only time we have the right to feel like we're "enough" is when we have won the approval of a person or a group of people, whether it's the approval of our parents, our teachers, our employers, our government, or our religion.

We've been taught that we must work to deserve the feeling of being enough. This is a myth that must be destroyed and destroyed now, because it creates a never-ending feeling of inadequacy, rather than a never-ending feeling of joy—and you were created to experience joy!

You don't have to work to be what you already are, but you may need to work on becoming aware of it.

If you work to get the approval of someone other than yourself, it won't be long before their approval needs to be bigger and more inspiring, or you'll need someone new you can impress so you'll have a new influx of approval. We don't do this because we are bad people but because along the way we have never really approved of ourselves. Somewhere along the line, we agreed with other people's appraisal of us, or we succumbed to our own faulty self-appraisal, and lived as if these appraisals were telling us something that should not be challenged, something that is true whether we like it or not. Not only *can* these appraisals be challenged, they must be challenged and changed if we are going to live happy lives.

People who do not accept themselves as being complete just because they exist are vulnerable in two areas: first, they will always be looking for validation from something outside themselves, needing acceptance, compliments, and recognition, rather than getting these things as the natural response that comes from expressing completeness. And second, they will allow what other people think to be more important than what they think. This state of mind is never satisfied, for it has within itself a deep hole that can never be filled. That hole is called: *I'm not enough*. I'm not smart enough. I'm not pretty enough. I'm not educated enough … and so on.

The cycle of not feeling like we're enough must be deliberately broken. The best way to do that is to realize that the Source of our being is Life, and Life is always enough. The challenge is to express our enough-ness.

Rosa Parks is one of the best examples of someone who knew she was enough and had the courage to express it. Her story is now a part of American history. Forty years ago, Ms. Parks refused to give up her seat on a bus in Montgomery, Alabama, to a white man because she was tired and weary from a long day at work. In an interview conducted by Kira Albin, Ms. Albin writes, " ... there's a misconception here that does not do justice to the woman whose act of courage began turning the wheels of the civil rights movement. Rosa Parks was physically tired, but no more than you or I after a long day's work. In fact, under other circumstances, she would have probably given up her seat to a child or elderly person. But this time, Parks was tired of the treatment that she and other African Americas received every day of their lives, what with racism, segregation, and the Jim Crow laws of the time."

Ms. Parks revealed something quite wonderful in her book *Quiet Strength* when she wrote, "I think it should be just history, period, and not thinking in terms of black history month." In her own way, I believe Ms. Parks is telling us that the issue of feeling incomplete runs rampant through all races, colors, and nationalities; and everyone is challenged to live as if they were sacred.

The American way of life is built on the premise that every person is born free and left free to live life as an individual, as long as no one is hurt in the process. What's interesting is that so many of us have chosen to use our freedom to bind ourselves to incompleteness. American culture made freedom sacred and this is good, but the only reason freedom is sacred is because people are sacred. We will never be free as a nation until we accept ourselves without reservation as individuals. The Declaration of Independence reads:

"We hold these truths to be self-evident, that all men are created equal, that they are endowed by their Creator with certain inalienable Rights, that among these are Life, Liberty and the pursuit of Happiness."

Every time the commercial world of advertising promises to make our hair brighter, our teeth whiter, our skin smoother, and our lives more worthy of envy, it promotes the idea that it holds the secret of enough-ness. Every time a religion promises to upgrade our position in the spiritual world because of something we did or did not do, it presents itself as the key holder to enough-ness. Every time we pursue Life, Liberty or Happiness outside of ourselves we are denying that we and we alone hold to key to fulfillment.

The best way to live life is to find a reason to feel good about being exactly who you are regardless of the circumstances that surround you. And the best reason is that you are life, and life is already complete.

In his book *The Hidden Power*, Thomas Troward writes, "To do any work successfully, you must believe yourself to be a whole man in respect of it. The completed work is an outward image of a corresponding completeness in yourself. We cannot successfully attempt *any* work until, for some reason or other, we believe ourselves to be able to accomplish it."

He goes on to say, "In forming man, the Creative Principle, must have produced a perfect work, and our conception of ourselves as imperfect can only be the result of our own ignorance of what we really *are*."

Nothing we can do or keep from doing can make us complete, because our completeness is part and parcel of our permanent identity; an identity that transcends the way we walk, talk, or look; an identity that transcends the wonderful things we have accomplished or plan to accomplish; an identity based on something far more substantial than what can be seen. An identity that is based on what we *are*.

This way of thinking may seem to undermine the importance of accomplishment. Some people may say, "Well, if we're enough, why bother doing anything? " The answer is simple: because we also need to experience our creative power.

It can all be reduced to this:

Life is an exercise in, first, remembering that we are complete, and then using that completeness to create the kind of life that satisfies us.

❋

CONSTRUCTIVE SELF-TALK:

I am living a complete life now. I'm not waiting for anyone or anything to make me complete, and it is out of my completeness that I can create the kind of life that pleases me.

THE JOY OF
ACCOMPLISHMENT

DOES OUR NATURE REQUIRE THAT WE MAKE a contribution to society? No. If we are complete, our nature requires nothing. Contributing to our own life experience or to society in general is entirely up to the individual, but a person's intrinsic worth is not dependent on the contribution they have made. Is Mother Teresa enough only because of the good she did in the world? Of course not! You may say, "You mean that there is no difference between Mother Teresa and me?" Yes, that's what I mean. Remember, sacredness is unconditional. It cannot be bought or sold, won or lost.

There may be a difference between what Mother Teresa *accomplished* and what you have accomplished, and there may be a difference between what Mother Teresa represents to society and what you represent, but there is no difference in the essential self of either of you. You are both life's perfect expression of itself. Surely Mother Teresa knew this, and that's exactly why she helped people without question. She made it her business to relate to people as if they were complete.

Somewhere along the line, we have come to believe that the rich owe something to the poor, that they should give something back to society. Why? If the rich created their wealth legally, why is anything owed to anyone? Wealth is not what makes a person complete, and neither does being generous.

Contributing to society in any way is a gift. Period.

In 1995 the man who created the vaccine that conquered one of the world's most devastating diseases, died. The disease was polio, and those who lived through this epidemic can remember things like iron lungs, the March of Dimes, and not being able to go swimming in the summer. Our hero's name, of course, is Dr. Jonas Salk. An interesting thing about Dr. Salk is that, though he became a world celebrity overnight, he never received the Nobel Prize.

What's the lesson here? The most important lesson comes from Dr. Salk's own lips. He said, "I've learned enough in my life to know that I must go my own way."

When we're operating from a deep understanding of life, we do what we do not to get accolades or to be thought of as a hero, but because it is simply ours to do. And it's ours to do because we say it's ours to do.

Dr. Salk said, "You can only fail if you stop too soon." *The Los Angeles Times* wrote, "This statement is vintage Salk–stubborn, independent, determined to do things his own way."

Go your own way when it comes to life. If you agree with the tenets of a philosophy or religion make them your own. You don't have to agree with everything a person thinks to enjoy that person's company, and you don't have to agree with everything that a philosophy or religion stands for, to benefit from it.

Get used to knowing the difference between the letter and the spirit of things.

Every time you create something that is the result of your own conscious efforts, acknowledge it. You would not have been successful if you had not embodied the end result in some way, consciously or unconsciously. Talk to yourself and tell yourself this is true, because it is.

Don't give in to the idea that you can't do what you want to do. Polio might still be a problem if

Salk talked to himself this way. Remember, your experience of life is the result of what your mind does to itself. You were born to express and experience the Life Force, to give and receive, to love and be loved. You were born to celebrate life by participating *in* it and benefiting *from* it.

There's nothing wrong with feeling great because you've accomplished something; just remember, even the greatest accomplishment doesn't change the nature of your being.

In other words, let yourself—yes, *encourage* yourself—to feel good about what you accomplish, but don't think that what you have accomplished makes you more of what you *are*. That's the trap! Completeness can't be bought or sold, won or lost. Completeness is! Nothing we can think, say or do, can add to what we are; it can only add to our experience of life.

CONSTRUCTIVE SELF-TALK:

*I enjoy knowing that I can accomplish what
I set out to do but I never forget that what I am,
is always more important than what I do.*

GOD

BY NOW, I'M SURE YOU'VE NOTICED that I have tried to avoid the word *God*. Instead, I've used words like Life Force, the Transcendent Self and the Sacred Self.

People have two reactions to the word *God*. They are reminded either of a vengeful person who is keeping tabs on them or of something they gave up long ago–religion!

The word *God* turns a lot of people off. It did me. But that was because I had been taught to believe in a Sky God who lived either to punish or reward me, and either by grace or eternal damnation I would end up in heaven or hell.

One thing I was sure of, I was headed for hell. Why? Well, I assumed that I had never really pleased God, so why at the end would God invite me into heaven? Well, time passed and I eventually became an atheist to both this heaven and this God, and I remained an atheist all through my Air Force days and many years after, only to eventually discover the real God: the transcendent self of me–a self that has the ability to rise above conditions and create new ones because it lives inside of the Source of all Power and the Source of Power lives inside of it.

Let's clarify an important point: I am not saying that I am God, The Life Force; I am saying I *individualize* God. I individualize the Life Force. I am the point at which the completeness of life finds expression. This means, I am God-in-action.

I can express this completeness in wonderful ways or in less than wonderful ways, but regardless of the way I express this Divine completeness, I am nonetheless complete. In other words, my identity cannot be changed by what I do or don't do.

I am Life's perfect expression of itself, and in this sense, I am the God of my own experience and you are the God of yours. If you don't like the word God, for Gods sake, find a word that describes the feeling of being enough.

Author Ernest Holmes wrote, " I give thanks to the God that *is*, that the God that is *thought to be* isn't."

CONSTRUCTIVE SELF-TALK:

I individualize Life, therefore I am enough.

YOUR ENOUGH-NESS
IS CREATIVE

"I know of no more encouraging fact than the unquestionable ability of a man to elevate his life by means of a conscious endeavor."

– HENRY DAVID THOREAU

WE CREATE BY MEANS of the sum total of everything that is going on in our minds. Our thoughts, attitudes, beliefs, opinions, and feelings all combine to form our consciousness and it is our consciousness that determines our experience.

What we consciously or *un*consciously develop in consciousness (our minds) appears in our lives in one way or another.

There are people who are famous, or should I say infamous, for using the power of their own minds in a terribly destructive way, and people famous for using that same power in wonderful ways. The power never changes. Only our use of it changes.

One use of power is to decide that we don't have what it takes to have a career that makes us happy, because our resume isn't good enough, or there just aren't enough jobs to go around, or no one really appreciates what we have to offer. It's pretty obvious that we are developing something we won't like. That's why we tell someone who is thinking this way to stop it. At some level, we all know that there is a connection between our experience of life and the way we use our mind.

That connection is one of cause and effect. What's going on in our mind is cause. What's going on in our experience is effect. You can't have one without the other.

We can use our enough-ness to create success or failure, but neither identifies us. Success and failure are just experiences that we, as creative beings, have the power to cause. You are not your successes nor are you your failures. You are life, and life is greater than the way it shows up in the world.

Descartes wrote these now famous words, "I think, therefore I am." The founder of Divine Science, Melinda Cramer, made this change. "I am, therefore I think."

We are not creative beings by choice. We are creative by nature and there's nothing we can do about it.

CONSTRUCTIVE SELF-TALK:

I am creative because I can think.

THE TRANSFERENCE
OF POWER

WHEN WE WERE YOUNG, we were under the rule of adults. When it came to power, they had it and we didn't. They made most of the decisions in the family, including decisions that affected us, until we could make those decisions for ourselves. This is what family life is all about. As we matured, however, we got a little anxious about wanting our own power. We wanted to make our own decisions. It's called growing up. Since power is a mental thing, the transfer of power is a mental act.

If we have made this transference of power and located it within our own mind, we will never relate to other people as if *they* represent the power in our life. We may listen to other people's opinions, but in the end we will make our own decisions and accept the responsibility that goes with them.

This may take getting used to, but it has to be done if we are to live according to our own nature.

The problems that occur between teenagers and their parents are often caused by a struggle for power, a struggle for independence. If the parent realizes that this struggle is natural, the parents can then teach the child about the responsibility that comes with personal power, making the transition from living at home to moving away much easier.

What is the primary payoff of not transferring power to the self? We always have someone to blame for things not working out right. When we accept responsibility for being the sole power in our own lives, we have no one to blame not even ourselves. Instead of blame, we take responsibility. There is a big difference between the two.

When we first learn that we are the cause of what's happening in our lives, we often blame ourselves for having used the creative principle in a destructive way. What's wrong with this picture? It reveals that we do not realize that the creative principle is always responding to what's going on in our minds, even when we are blaming ourselves for something.

You can't blame yourself for something without feeling bad; whereas taking responsibility often inspires. It's the difference between reacting to life from a place of power or a place of powerlessness.

Because we have caused so many of our experiences *unconsciously*, taking responsibility makes much more sense than self-blame.

❀

CONSTRUCTIVE SELF-TALK:

I honor and respect all people. I never forget that I am the only power in my life.

I take responsibility for my life by reacting to everything and everyone in a constructive way.

TAKING
RESPONSIBILITY

OUR FUTURE IS UNDER NO OBLIGATION other than to respond to what we are thinking now. If we take responsibility for what we allow our mind to think about, believe, and feel now ... we will undoubtedly be creating a wonderful future. If we don't, we won't. Is this hard to do? Whether it is or not, it must be done.

Traditionally, teachers of this mental science have told us that we cannot create something new until we take full responsibility for having caused what exists now. Though this is one approach to this science, it is not the only approach.

Another approach is to realize that what's important is what happens from this point forward, not what happened up until now. If I take charge of my mind now, taking full responsibility for what happens from here on out, what difference does it make if I take responsibility for what happened before?

The important thing is to take responsibility for being the one in charge of all change from this point forward, taking responsibility for the way we think and feel from this point on.

It's okay to say, "I just can't accept that I caused all the terrible things that have happened to me." Whether you did or didn't cause them, you are cause now and the only thing you need to affirm is: "I am in charge of what happens to me from now on."

Taking responsibility requires strength of character, because there may be times when we are tempted to blame someone else for what's happening to us or when it just doesn't seem possible that what needs to change is our own consciousness. This is called taking loving responsibility, and it means that we don't blame anyone, including ourselves, for what's happening.

You see, the act of taking responsibility can easily turn into self-punishment if it includes self-blame. No one feels good when they place blame on themselves. That's why taking *loving* responsibility is so necessary.

Never use blame as a way to rise above conditions. If you are blaming someone for something in your life, you are not rising above conditions, you are avoiding something.

Instead, take loving responsibility from this day forward. If there is something in your mind that you need to change, change it without making anyone wrong, including yourself.

There's an old saying "You can't know where you're going, if you don't know where you've been." Not true. To get where you're going all you need to know is where that is and how you're going to get there, and then to start moving in that direction. When we're driving, we don't use our rear-view mirror to tell us where we're going, so the main thing we have to take responsibility for is doing what is necessary to cause the future that we desire.

The Life Force in you is bigger than any condition you may be facing, so rise above it by taking loving responsibility for being cause to the masterpiece you are now in the process of creating.

CONSTRUCTIVE SELF-TALK:
I take loving responsibility for my life.

SHAME

SHAME IS THE BIGGEST BLOCK TO LIVING a happy life. It makes us hide from people, circumstances and even ourselves. Shame comes in all shapes and sizes, and affects people in many different ways. Some people let themselves be shamed by their sexuality, while others are ashamed of their height, weight, color, religious affiliation, a family member, or a past experience. We can even feel shame because we are not the "best" at something.

I once counseled a woman who spent no less than ten years carrying around what she felt was the shame of being divorced, because she was raised to believe that it is up to the woman to keep a marriage together; and if a marriage falls apart, the wife is always to blame.

The list of shame-issues is endless. I know a minister who one day realized that her church wasn't growing because of the shame she felt toward her mother, who was a drinker and a member of her church. The minister believed that her mother's drinking reflected something about her ministry. When this minister realized that what her mother did or didn't do did not reflect on her or her ministry, she gave up shame and her church grew.

Some people let their entire lives be affected by their shame, while others let certain parts of their lives be affected.

The thing to know about shame is that it is always self-imposed. Even if someone else tries to shame us, we are the ones who have the last word. We can refuse to feel shame or we can submit to it, deluding ourselves into believing that we are doing something right.

Shame is never right, for it inhibits the life force from expressing freely. Shame binds us to the experience we feel ashamed about instead of freeing us to experience our enough-ness.

While shame may keep some people from doing something illegal, dishonest, immoral, or unethical, in most cases it doesn't. In most cases shame robs us of remembering that we are enough.

If you have inadvertently put your picture next to the word *shame* in your mental dictionary, take it out right now and put it instead next to the word *love*.

CONSTRUCTIVE SELF-TALK:

*I refuse to experience shame, accept shame,
or shame anyone else, because shame doesn't add,
it subtracts from life.*

YOUR IDENTITY

WE CAN CHANGE THE WAY WE THINK about ourselves, but we do not have the power to change our
actual identity. Like it or not, we are each a complete
being, and there's nothing we can do about it. One
day we may think of ourselves as capable of dealing
with life and the next day incapable, but the Truth is,
regardless of appearances or the way we feel or what
we are thinking, we are one with all the power in the
Universe, therefore always capable. This is the
nature of Reality, and it's non-negotiable.

Never identify yourself at the level of your experience, even if your experience is wonderful. You are
bigger than even the best of human experiences. So,
of course, you are bigger than the least.

Yes, identity is a major issue in life. Your real
identity cannot be won and can never be lost,
because it is forged out of life itself. You are not your
body, your clothes, your accomplishments or the

experiences you have had. You are not even your awareness. You are that which creates awareness. You are an individualization of the highest expression of life, the human mind ... and as such have the power to create the kind of life you desire, because the human mind is Divine.

The creative power that resides in your mind is your mind, which means the experiences you will have will be the result of what your mind does to itself. Remember, experiences don't change themselves. Mind changes experiences. You are worth more than you will ever experience, but you will only experience what you think you're worth. Jesus said, "It is done unto you as you believe." I believed that a middle-class Polish American boy would never amount to much. I experienced my belief but I also transcended it. So can you! How? By taking responsibility for being the one in charge ... of what you think, what you feel, and what you believe, and most of all—the way you identity yourself.

CONSTRUCTIVE SELF-TALK:

I am a complete being and I like it.
I'm ready to take charge of my life by taking
charge of the way I use my mind.

THINKING

MORE THAT ANY OTHER MENTAL ACTIVITY, we think and our thinking is what determines practically everything else. You see life the way you do because you think, feel, and believe in your own particular way. The thing to remember however is that you are the thinker not the thought, the believer not the belief, the one who feels not the feeling. What goes on in your mind doesn't identify you. It only identifies the way you are using your mind to perceive life. You are in charge of what goes on in your mind, therefore you are in charge of the way you perceive life and only you can change your perception.

Did you ever think badly of someone you've never met because you'd heard bad things about them, and then meet them, only to change what you think? Of course. There was good reason to change your mind, and you did.

When we discover that our thought is creative,

we have good reason not to think negatively about ourselves or anyone else for that matter. Instead, we think thoughts that acknowledge the great truth that regardless of the way someone *expresses* life, that someone is complete. This is also true about us. A person's thought may not reflect this completeness, neither may their experience, but the essential self, the experience-maker, the thing that person *is* … is complete.

CONSTRUCTIVE SELF-TALK:

The only thoughts I think are the ones that make me feel good about myself and the world I live in.

FEELING

LET'S TAKE FEELING NEXT. Don't tell yourself that you just can't help the way you feel. Of course you can. We feel the way we do because we think the way we do. The next time you feel a little depressed, ask yourself what's been going on in your mind recently. You will most probably discover that you've been thinking thoughts like: "Why me?" "I'm being taken advantage of." "Nobody appreciates me."

Immediately take responsibility for these thoughts. Tell yourself that you could be thinking other thoughts if you wanted to, and then think them. Replace the old thoughts with: "Regardless of the way it's been up until now, from now on I appreciate myself; and because I do, others do too." "I feel good about being exactly who I am." "I'm ready to change what needs to be changed in my mind, so I can move forward." "I am enough right now. I know it. I feel it and I love it."

Once it dawns on you that your thinking is creative, know that you can think what you should be thinking and you can keep from thinking what you shouldn't think. And make the issue that simple. This is called self-talk and self-talk is the key to your future.

CONSTRUCTIVE SELF-TALK:

I feel good because of the way I use my mind.

BELIEVING

WE NOW NEED TO TAKE A LOOK AT BELIEVING and how our beliefs, working in tandem with what we think and feel, shape our experience. We believe the things we do because our mind has come to certain conclusions, and we call those conclusions ... what we know or what we believe. We formed those conclusions by consciously or unconsciously combining everything going on in our mind. Most of our beliefs have been unconsciously formed. I never sat down and consciously decided to come to a conclusion about my ability to tap dance, but now that I think of it, I have one such conclusion: I can't do it. I have unconsciously reached a conclusion. Is it something I believe or something I know?

Don't quibble over whether your conclusions represent something you "know" or something you "believe." The important thing is that it's something that you have internalized, regardless of what you call it.

We have beliefs about absolutely everything that our mind has entertained. My mind has never entertained the types of fabric used in clothing worn in North Africa, so I have no belief about them. If information about this fabric enters my mind, I am apt to form either an opinion about it or a belief about it. The more information we have about something, the more likely we are to make intelligent decisions in regard to it.

We are told, "It is done unto us as we believe." Is this true? I think the issue is bigger than what we believe. What's important is the sum total of everything that is going on in our mind, which includes our thoughts, feelings, beliefs, attitudes, and even our opinions. All of these combined form our consciousness, and it's our consciousness that determines our experience.

You believe the things you do because you have consciously or unconsciously accepted certain ideas, to the exclusion of their opposite. You either believe you are complete or you believe that you are incomplete, but you can't believe you are both at the same time.

The interesting thing about what's going on in our mind is that everything matches. Our opinions usually match what we believe, and so do our attitudes.

The smart person checks his or her own mind on a regular basis to see whether or not what's going on is healthy. If, it is not, they change it by replacing it with what *is* healthy. The most effective way to do this is to become aware of our own self-talk and use it to talk our way into another frame of mind. This is best done by using the power of repetition.

CONSTRUCTIVE SELF-TALK:

My beliefs are based on ideas that are healthy-minded. If I discover thoughts that do not support my highest good, I change them into thoughts that do.

SELF-TALK

THE ACTIVITY THAT FILLS MOST OF EVERYONE'S DAY is self-talk and the kind of self-talk we do is the result of what we have mentally embraced. If we have embraced fear, our self-talk is fear-driven. If we have embraced faith, our self-talk is faith-driven.

Most people don't give much importance to Self-Talk because they do it all the time; it's silent, it's private, and besides, "I have the right to think what I want to think."

Don't hide behind your rights, come out and discover the way the Spiritual System is constructed, so you can play the game of life and have some fun doing it. The main reason that people don't think Self-Talk is important is that it doesn't *seem* significant, it doesn't *feel* important. All mental activity is important. But self-talk is the *most* important, because we do it *all* the time! We spend more time in self-talk than we do in any spiritual practice.

Is self-talk important only because we do it all the time? No. Self-talk is important because it is the main contributor to consciousness. Take a step back from what's going on in your mind and listen to what it's saying. You may be surprised. You may be saying things like, *I can accomplish anything I set my mind to*, or you may be saying, *I've never really accomplished much of anything; why now, all of a sudden, do I think I can?* You may be saying, *she makes me feel so stupid*, or maybe you've been saying, *I have been letting her opinion of me mean more than what I know to be true.* Raymond Charles Barker tells us what is true in his book *The Power of Decision*: "You were born as Intelligence in a universe of Intelligence, to unfold, evolve and create as Intelligence."

Decide right now to talk to yourself in a way that makes you feel good about being who you are, about being enough, about being able to accomplish whatever you set out to do. And don't take no for an answer. If your mind finds exceptions to these great truths, intercede on your own behalf and refuse to accept them. The truth about you is true whether you know it or not, like it or not, or even accept it or not. Get tough with yourself. Don't accept ideas that undermine your identity as an integral part of the Life Force, no matter where these ideas come from.

CONSTRUCTIVE SELF-TALK:

*My self-talk is constructive
because I want more out of life.*

THE POWER OF
REPETITION

SELF-TALK IS IMPORTANT, AND REPETITION is the key. It's what we say to ourselves all the time that counts, not just once in a while. If most of our self-talk acknowledges our completeness, we will feel good about being who we are; but if most of our self-talk denies our completeness, we will not feel equipped to meet the demands that life makes upon us, let alone the demands we make on ourselves.

Remember, you are not trying to convince anyone, including the Life Force, that you are enough or that you can accomplish what you set out to do. You are in the process of convincing yourself, and that may take some doing. Why? Well, whether you remember it or not, it took some doing to convince you that you weren't enough to begin with. Now, you must be willing to invest in yourself, spending whatever time is necessary to convince yourself of what has always been true.

Be willing to use the power of repetition as you talk to yourself. Let your mind hear over and over again, from you, that you have what it takes, that you were created by a Life Force that requires your participation in what Noel Coward calls the Human Holiday. As Emerson writes, "Absolve you to yourself, and you shall have the suffrage of the world." We will not satisfy our souls until we convince ourselves that we are worthwhile because we exist. And when that happens, the world will respond because it must.

CONSTRUCTIVE SELF-TALK:

I am willing to have a constructive influence on myself and have it all the time, not just occasionally.

SO WHAT!

OUR TENDENCY TO PUNISH OURSELVES seems endless. If we don't feel like we meet the world as a complete being, if we don't approve of something we did or didn't do, we punish ourselves ... if in no other way, than by just feeling bad. And the interesting thing is that it seems as if feeling bad makes up for the bad thing we think we did. We believe that at some level, feeling bad equalizes the universe of cause and effect. But it doesn't. Feeling bad can never be justified when you realize that, as a transcendent being, you are bigger than what makes you feel bad. Instead of feeling bad, say, "so what!"

The words *so what!* can be the most healing words you will ever speak, if they represent the relinquishment of the excuses for why things haven't worked out well and the embodiment of ideas that cause things to work out well. If *so what!* represents a mind that refuses to deal with an issue, these words won't heal. They are just avoiding the issue.

When Dr. Salk was presented with the idea that the polio virus had spread to Europe, New Zealand, and Australia, which it had, I can imagine him saying, "So what! Now let's get to work and create a vaccine that cures it." Saying "so what!" then isn't a flippant statement that says we don't care about something. It's a response that shows we are not going to let anything keep us from taking constructive action. If you can say "so what!" about something, you're done with it.

If your self-talk has been negative, so what! Change it. And make the issue that simple. It's better to get rid of negative thoughts than it is to admonish the thinker. If you've failed at practically everything you've ever attempted, so what! You have proven that you are creative. Not get busy and create again.

Let no experience keep you from accepting yourself without reservation. If you grew up with very little love, so what! The love you give is more important than the love you get, so choose to make up for the love you didn't get by giving the love you've been withholding all these years. It's your turn.

You are not finished with an experience until you can look at it and say:

So what! I am not going to waste my time feeling bad about what I said or did, or what happened to me, because I am busy embodying the quality of life I wish to experience from this moment forward.

I refuse to scold myself; instead I acknowledge my ability to transcend and move on.

Saying "so what!" isn't a flip remark that refuses to take responsibility for causing something. It's the remark of a mind that knows that what it focuses on, it creates. So what! changes focus from the past so you can focus on the present. If you lost your job, so what! Should you feel bad about it? What good will that do? Should you feel like you've been cheated? Again, what good will that do? Saying "so what!" frees you to move forward.

So what! may not be the most effective way to respond to other people, because they'll probably think you're being a smart-arse, but it is an effective way to talk to yourself.

Saying "so what!" also doesn't excuse you from apologizing when an apology is due. If you need to make an apology, make it and be sincere about it, but don't let making an apology diminish you. As the saying goes, "It takes a big man to apologize." So what! is a way to let go of the negative and embrace the positive.

If you have disappointed yourself along the way, so what! Rather than scold yourself, acknowledge your ability to move on.

CONSTRUCTIVE SELF-TALK:

Instead of scolding myself, I engage my ability to transcend what I have thought, said or done, and I move on.

NO MORE EXCUSES

IF WE DON'T SAY "SO WHAT!" we will probably arm ourselves with an excuse or two for why things haven't worked out the way we wanted them to. Excuses are deadly. They don't injure our desires, they kill them, because they replace them. If you have an excuse as to why you are not demonstrating greater good in your life, that's the reason you haven't. You have an excuse.

We have a choice. Shall we hold the vision of the completed idea in our mind, or shall we hold an excuse that explains why our idea hasn't yet taken form?

Let no excuse, no matter how logical it seems, be more important than proving your ability to bring an idea through to complete manifestation. And if someone asks you if you have fulfilled your desires as yet, have no excuse. If you feel you have to reply, say something like, "It's all taking form, or "It's all in process," or "Oh, shut up!" (just kidding)

What you say to someone else in regard to what you're working on is not as important as what you say to yourself. Again, self-talk.

You don't want a good excuse at the end of the day, you want fulfillment.

That means, give up the excuse, because if you don't, you just might let the excuse make you feel enough, and that's not why you're enough. You're enough because you exist, and don't you forget it!

CONSTRUCTIVE SELF-TALK:

*I drop all of my excuses
and focus on fulfillment instead.*

I REQUIRE

THE PERSON WHO REALIZES THE POWER of words will want to use words that reflect the highest truth. The Truth is that God doesn't want, or need, or yearn for anything. Great! This means, in my enough-ness, I don't want, need, or yearn for anything either, for I individualize God. How can I make my life better, then, if I don't want it to be better?

The key is to stop wanting, and start *requiring*. It's not so much that we want something, as that we *require* an experience that is equal to what we are accepting ourselves as being. If money is the issue, I might affirm:

I *require* prosperity because God is prosperous and I am one with God.

Now, who are we talking to? We're talking to ourselves. We give up telling ourselves what we want and need and even deserve, and start telling ourselves what we require, now that we know that our enough-ness has within it every good thing.

Requiring is the act of calling on the inner qualities of a perfect self to become visible in the outer world of form.

And remember, we don't get what we deserve, we get what we have mentally embodied. You deserve what you can cause by right of consciousness.

I discovered the word *require* as a replacement for words like *need* and *want* when I was a singer. I was playing the Vapors Club in Hot Springs, Arkansas, and was invited to the home of a lovely lady in her eighties for dinner. I accepted and was overwhelmed by the grand style in which the evening unfolded. She was obviously from the old school of gracious living. The dinnerware rivaled Hyacinth Bucket's Royal Doulton, and the table was set with more silverware than I had ever seen. At the end of the meal, the lady served coffee and asked, "David, do you require cream?" I thought to myself, I like cream, I always have cream, but I'm not sure I *require* cream. Then I thought again and realized that if there is no cream available, I don't drink coffee, so yes, I *require* cream.

This is the day when I replaced the words need, *want*, and *yearn*, with *require*. I require cream. And because I am conscious that I am complete, I require everything that goes with completeness.

I don't need money. I require it. I don't need to be successful, I require it.

I don't need love in my life. I require it. Not because I am incomplete, but because I know who I am.

I don't think we can *make* ourselves feel like we're complete or enough. We have to *let* ourselves feel enough, and this is because spiritual awareness cannot be forced. It has to evolve in its own way and at its own pace. "Sometimes, divine revelation simply means adjusting your brain to hear what your heart already knows."

There is something within you that knows you were meant to enjoy life, not to struggle through it, hoping that one day you would please God, your friends, and maybe even yourself.

You will please yourself the moment you stop thinking that you need something—anything—to become complete, and dare to accept your completeness now, just as things are. Let yourself feel good about being you and know that you require a life that is happy, healthy, and filled with the joy of life. You don't want these things, nor do you need them. You require them, because you know who you are.

CONSTRUCTIVE SELF-TALK:

I require everything that makes life worthwhile.

❀

THE PURPOSE
OF LIFE

I WAS RAISED TO BELIEVE THAT THE PURPOSE of life is to know, love, and serve God in this world, and to be happy with Him in the next. I no longer believe this. If happiness is important, it's important *now*.

Do I believe in reincarnation? Let's put it this way, I believe in immortality, that the spirit of every person lives on, in a way that most of us haven't trained ourselves to see. But I can't prove it.

Reincarnation usually refers to coming back to planet Earth and taking the form of a human being. I believe that the human holiday on planet Earth is just one choice. Surely, there must be more choices than one. In Albert Brooks' movie, *Defending Your Life*, there are many buses lined up taking people who have passed on to many different places to live out the next phase of eternity. Sounds right to me.

I don't believe that a person needs to believe in reincarnation or immortality to be happy. To be happy, a person needs to reckon with the spiritual values of this *parenthesis* in eternity, not the next, and the greatest spiritual value is the recognition that every person is enough because everyone is sacred ... everyone is of *God*.

The purpose of life is to strike a balance between acknowledging our completeness and enjoying our creativity.

CONSTRUCTIVE SELF-TALK:

My purpose in life is to be conscious of who I already am and aware of what I am able to accomplish.

THE CHOICE
IS YOURS

THE ONE IDEA EVERYONE SEEMS TO AGREE with is that since no one can do our thinking for us, we are free to believe what we want to believe. We can believe that our worth as human beings is tied to what we have made of ourselves, or that what we *are* is more important than what we accomplish. We must all make that decision for ourselves.

The great religions and philosophies of the world have told us what it means to be human. They have authored ideas that uplift and inspire, as well as ideas that depress and discourage. We have been told that we are worms of the dust, that we are sinners, and that there is no good thing in us, and we've also been told that we are sons and daughters of the Most High. We have been told that our basic nature is destructive, therefore we have to be taught how live in harmony with the rest of the world, and we've also been told that our basic nature is creative so we can overcome any obstacle that we set our minds to. We have been told to expect to suffer because we are human but that suffering is a good teacher.

Whether their words appear in the Bible or the *Wall Street Journal*, authors of doom and gloom do not believe there is much to be said in favor of the individual, except that maybe he has the ability to work hard and make something of himself if the devil doesn't get him first. This way of thinking overlooks the most important thing about being human:

Whether you make something of yourself or not, you are sacred because you exist. You matter because you exist.

CONSTRUCTIVE SELF-TALK:

I choose to think in a way that expresses my sacredness fully and completely.

BEING ENOUGH IS
JUST THE BEGINNING

To fully realize the power of enough-ness, you must understand that just merely accepting this concept is not the final step. On the contrary, it's the beginning. Knowing you are enough isn't a place to hide from life. The creative aspect of your nature needs to be exercised; therefore, your enough-ness is only a starting point.

Your enough-ness is an important starting point, because it establishes the nature of the creator in you as a complete being rather than someone who is trying to become complete by creating.

I cannot stress the importance of knowing the difference. The first approach feels good; the second approach is fraught with struggle.

It's who and what you get to be while you are accomplishing that makes life worthwhile.

✻

CONSTRUCTIVE SELF-TALK:

I am an individual.

No one has ever used their mind the way I have.

*No one has ever laughed or cried exactly the way
I have, and that's because there is only
one me for all time.*

*My life is balanced between acknowledging
my completeness and enjoying my creativity.*

*From this day forward I take charge of my mind,
what I think, what I feel, and what I believe.*

*My life will be what I make it, regardless
of the experiences I've had or am having.*

How wonderful it is ... to be enough!

CONCLUSION

Now that we have satisfied the yearning in our souls to understand our place in life, each of us can say, "I AM ENOUGH."

Having made this great discovery, we can now move forward and welcome the many challenges of life with a sense of joy, not competing with anyone else and not struggling to be "somebody," but accepting ourselves today, in this moment, just as we are.

This simple acceptance establishes the foundation, a starting point that we can build on. As we use our minds to create new and wonderful experiences, we remember that no experience can make us more of what we already are–an individualized expression of the life–of greater consequence than anything we will ever accomplish.

It's time to be enough.